Perplexing Picture Mazes

Conceptis Puzzles

STERLING

New York / London

www.sterlingpublishing.com

To find out more about Conceptis Puzzles,
visit www.conceptispuzzles.com.

STERLING and the distinctive Sterling logo are
registered trademarks of Sterling Publishing Co., Inc.

2 4 6 8 10 9 7 5 3

Published by Sterling Publishing Co., Inc.
387 Park Avenue South, New York, NY 10016
© 2007 by Conceptis Puzzles
Distributed in Canada by Sterling Publishing
c/o Canadian Manda Group, 165 Dufferin Street
Toronto, Ontario, Canada M6K 3H6
Distributed in the United Kingdom by GMC Distribution Services
Castle Place, 166 High Street, Lewes, East Sussex, England BN7 1XU
Distributed in Australia by Capricorn Link (Australia) Pty. Ltd.
P.O. Box 704, Windsor, NSW 2756, Australia

Sterling ISBN-13: 978-1-4027-5046-5
ISBN-10: 1-4027-5046-3

For information about custom editions, special sales, premium and
corporate purchases, please contact Sterling Special Sales Department
at 800-805-5489 or specialsales@sterlingpublishing.com.

Contents

Introduction

Solve a maze and create a picture! To start out, solve each of these fun puzzles just as you would a traditional maze: find the true path by starting at the maze's entrance and drawing a line to the maze's exit, avoiding false paths and dead ends. But the fun is not over once you exit! Color in the path you traced with a dark, thick line of pen or marker to create a picture.

You might be surprised to learn that picture mazes of this kind were invented in Japan over 20 years ago. Today picture mazes have a dedicated following among children and adults all over the world. So grab your marker and pencil and get started!

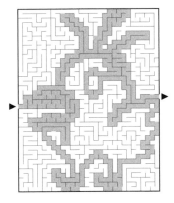

Maze #1

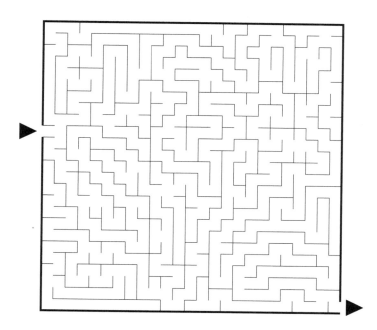

Maze #2

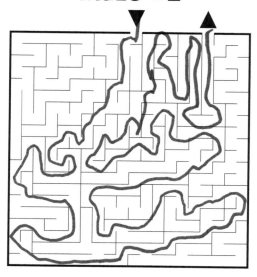

Solutions on page 78

5

Maze #3

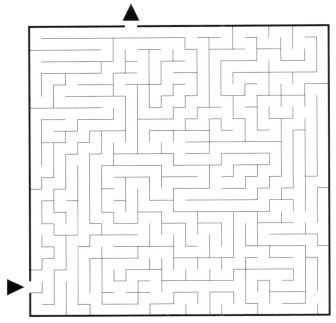

Maze #4

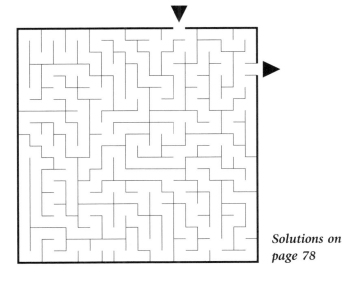

Solutions on page 78

Maze #5

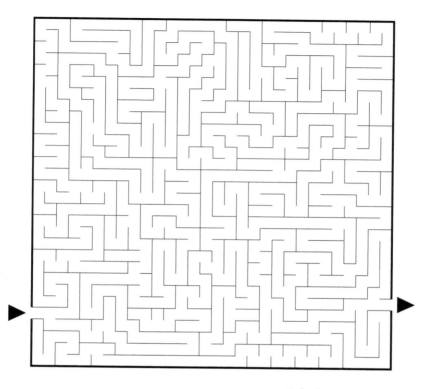

Solution on page 78

Maze #6

Solution on page 78

Maze #7

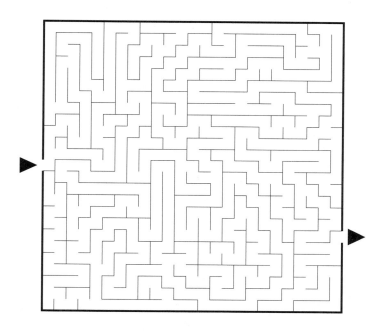

Maze #8

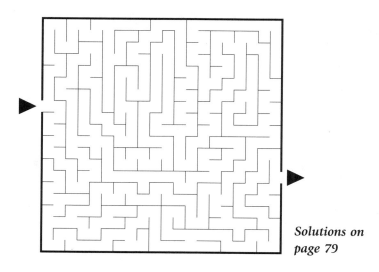

Solutions on page 79

Maze #9

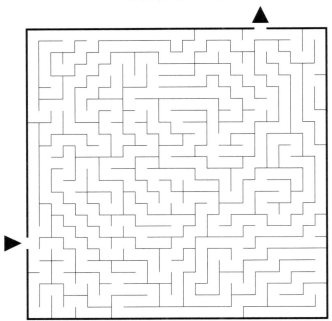

Maze #10

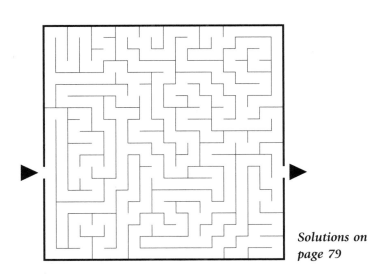

*Solutions on
page 79*

Maze #11

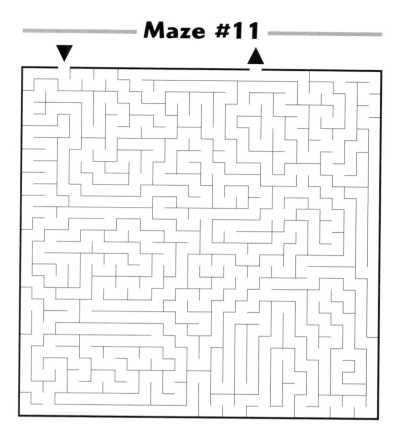

Solution on page 79

Maze #12

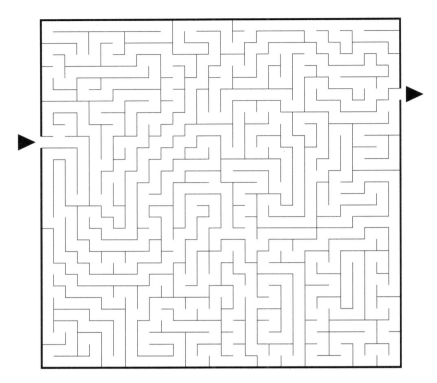

Solution on page 79

Solution on page 80

Maze #14

Solution on page 80

Solution on page 80

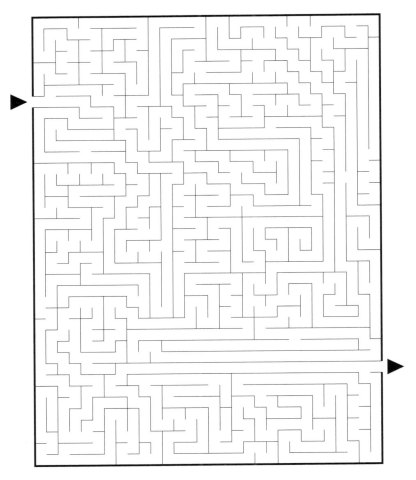

Solution on page 80

Solution on page 81

Maze #18

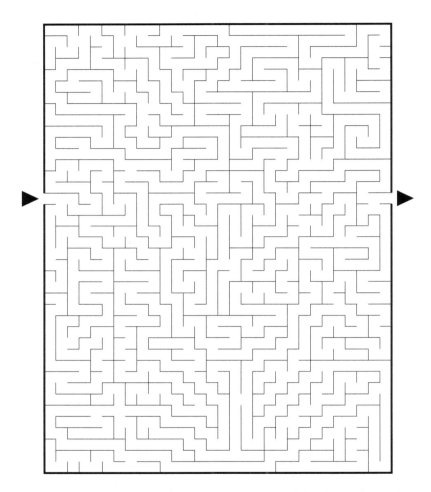

Solution on page 81

Maze #19

Solution on page 81

19

Solution on page 81

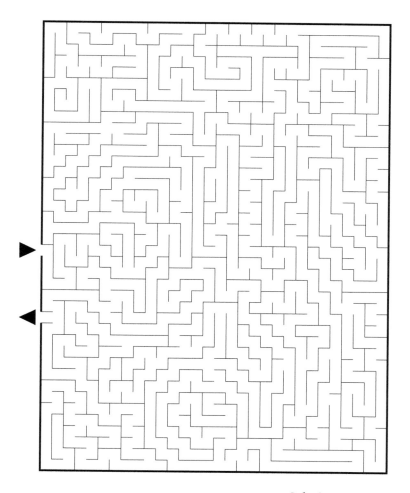

Solution on page 82

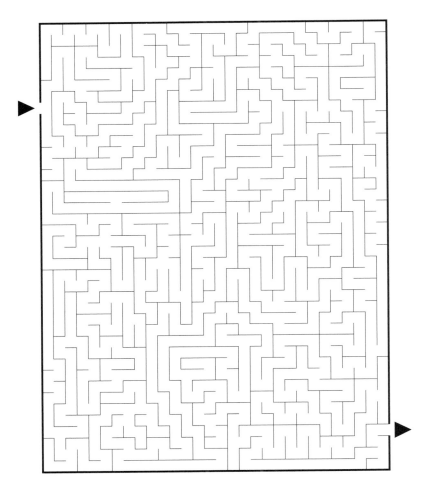

Solution on page 82

Solution on page 82

Maze #24

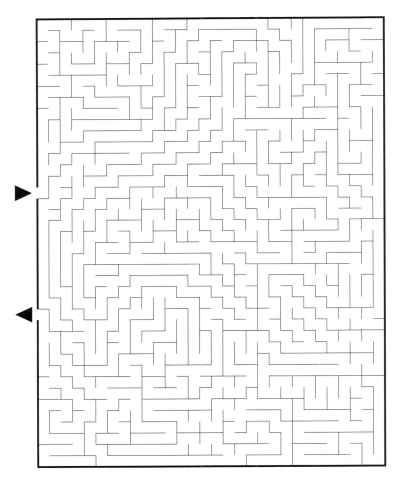

Solution on page 82

Solution on page 83

Solution on page 83

Solution on page 83

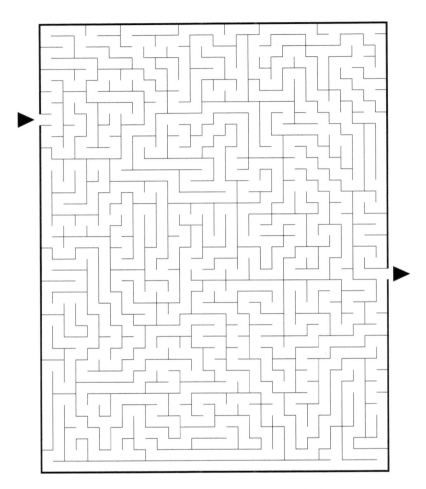

Solution on page 83

Solution on page 84

Solution on page 84

Solution on page 84

Solution on page 84

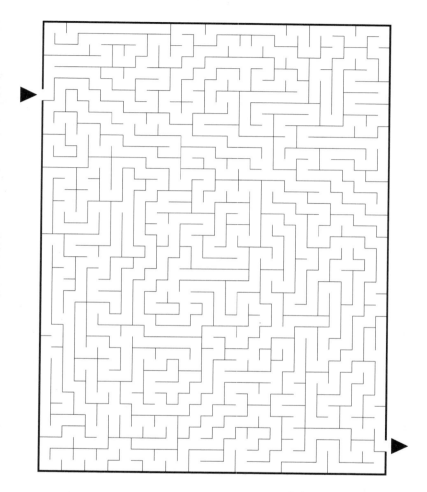

Solution on page 85

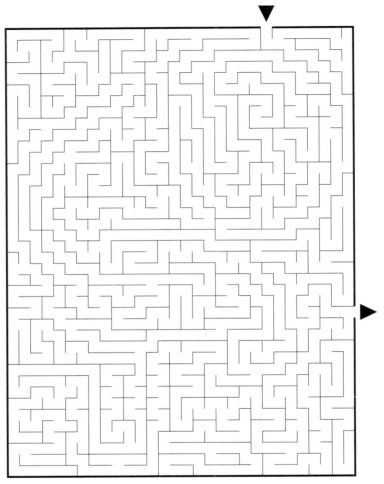

Solution on page 85

Maze #35

Solution on page 85

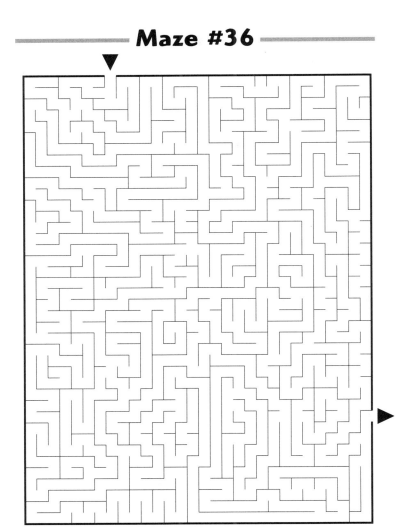

Solution on page 85

Solution on page 86

Maze #38

Solution on page 86

Maze #39

Solution on page 86

Solution on page 86

Maze #41

Solution on page 87

Maze #42

Solution on page 87

Maze #43

Solution on page 87

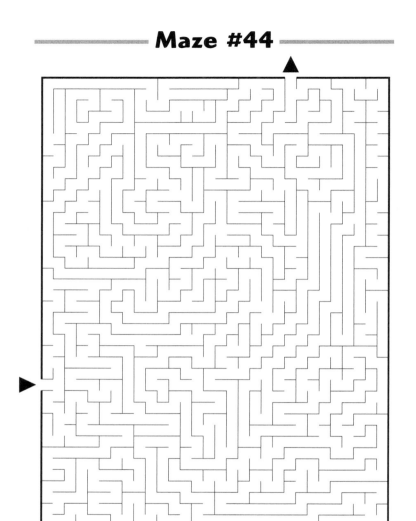

Solution on page 87

Maze #45

Solution on page 88

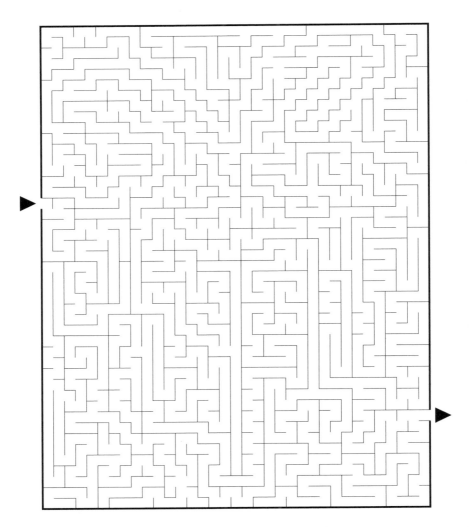

Solution on page 88

Maze #47

Solution on page 88

Solution on page 88

Solution on page 89

Maze #50

Solution on page 89

Solution on page 89

Maze #52

Solution on page 89

Solution on page 90

Maze #54

Solution on page 90

Solution on page 90

Maze #56

Solution on page 90

Maze #57

Solution on page 91

Solution on page 91

Maze #59

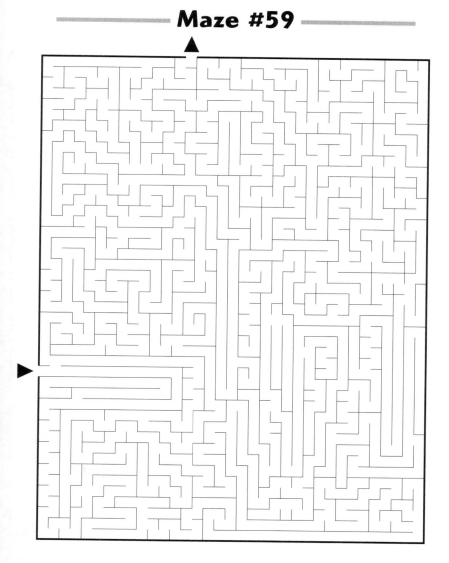

Solution on page 91

Solution on page 91

Solution on page 92

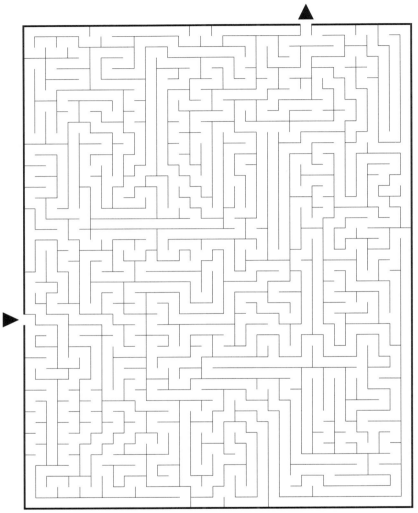

Solution on page 92

Solution on page 92

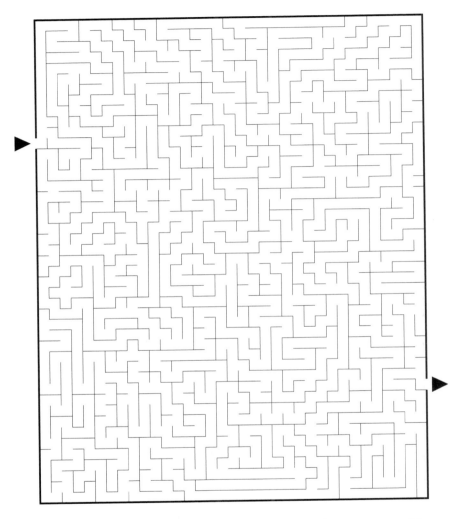

Solution on page 92

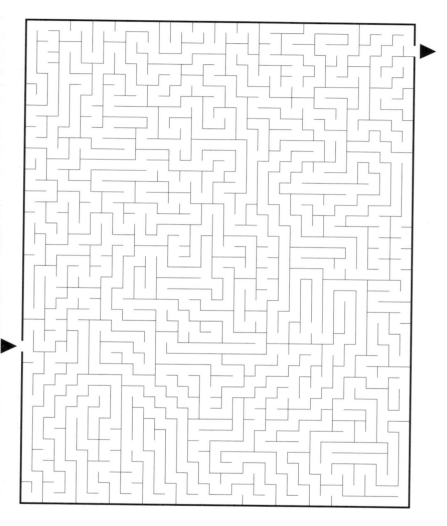

Solution on page 93

Solution on page 93

Maze #67

Solution on page 93

Solution on page 93

Solution on page 94

Maze #70

Solution on page 94

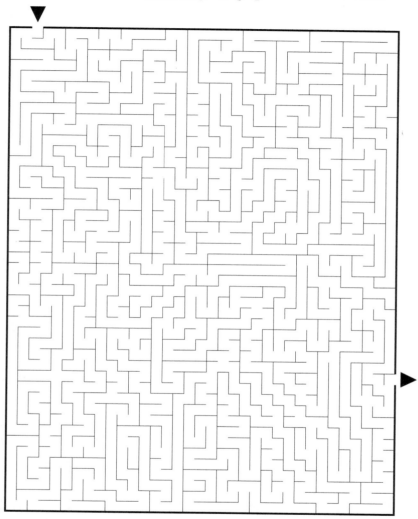

Solution on page 94

Solution on page 95

Solution on page 95

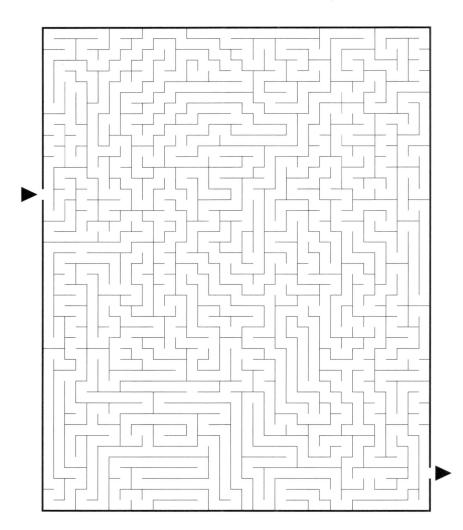

Solution on page 95

Solution on page 96

Maze #76

Solution on page 96

Solution on page 96

Solutions

Maze #1

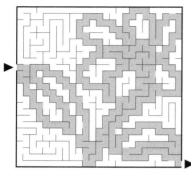

Maze #4

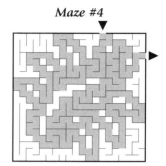

Maze #2

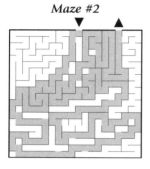

Maze #5

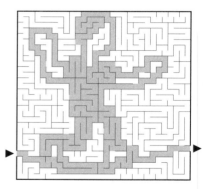

Maze #3

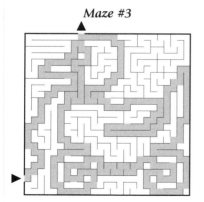

Maze #6

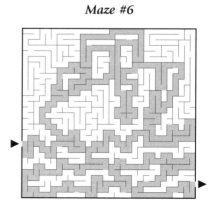

Solutions

Maze #10

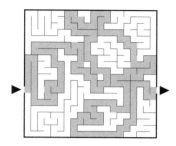

Maze #7

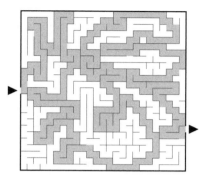

Maze #11

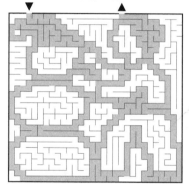

Maze #8

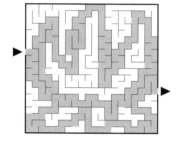

Maze #9

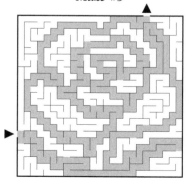

Maze #12

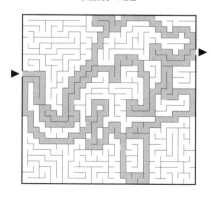

Solutions

Maze #15

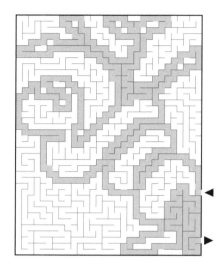

Maze #13

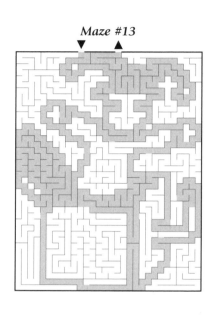

Maze #16

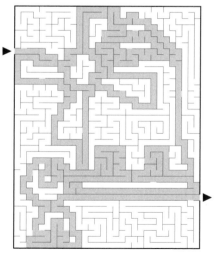

Maze #14

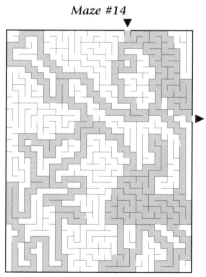

Solutions

Maze #17

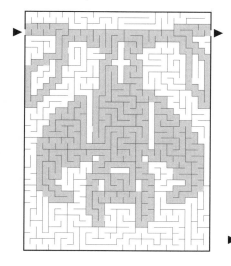

Maze #19

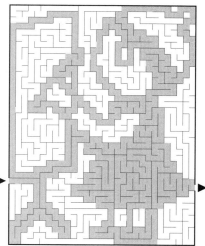

Maze #18

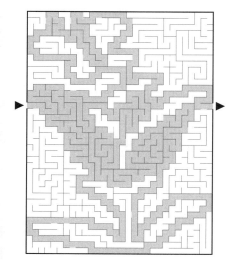

Maze #20

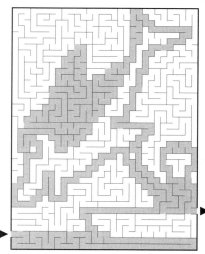

Solutions

Maze #21

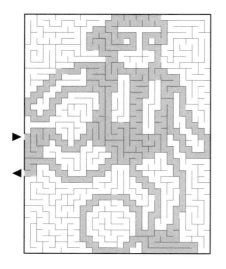

Maze #23

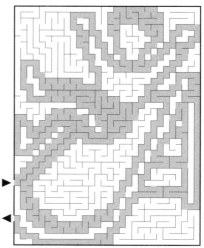

Maze #22

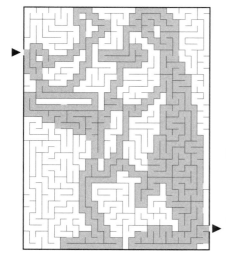

Maze #24

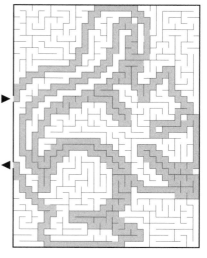

Solutions

Maze #27

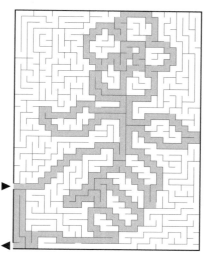

Maze #25

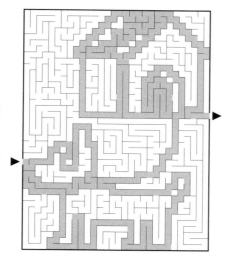

Maze #28

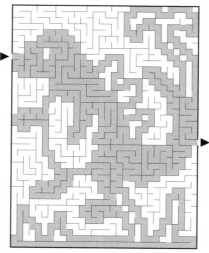

Maze #26

Solutions

Maze #29

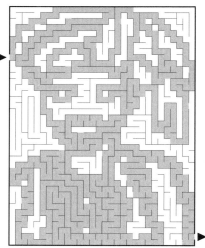

Maze #31

Maze #30

Maze #32

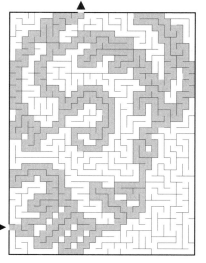

Solutions

Maze #35

Maze #33

Maze #34

Maze #36

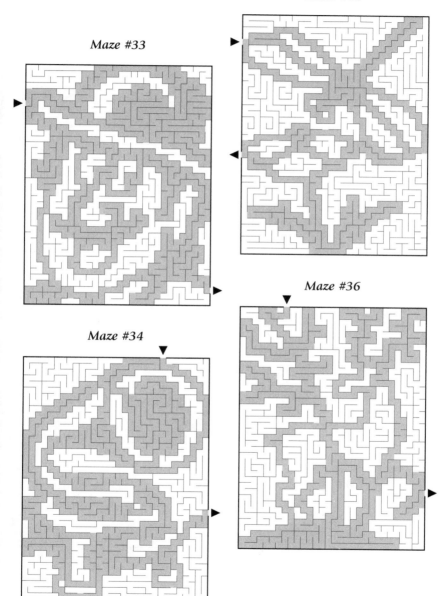

Solutions

Maze #39

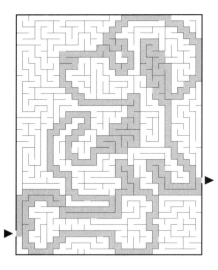

Maze #37

Maze #40

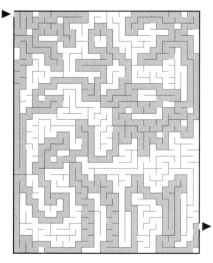

Maze #38

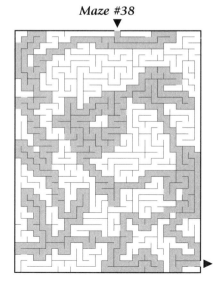

Solutions

Maze #41

Maze #43

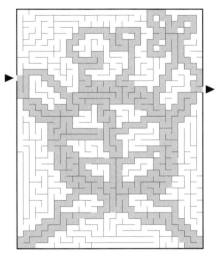

Maze #42

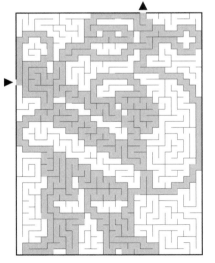

Maze #44

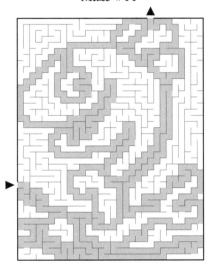

Solutions

Maze #45

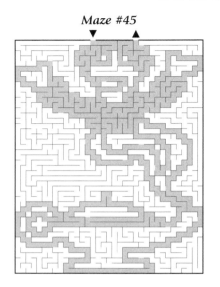

Maze #47

Maze #46

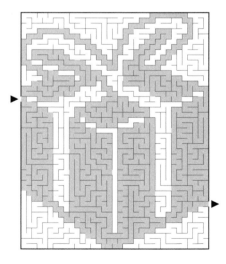

Maze #48

Solutions

Maze #51

Maze #49

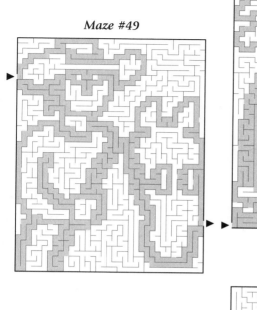

Maze #52

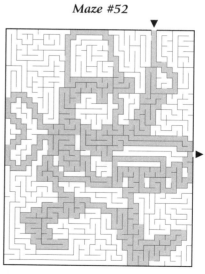

Maze #50

Solutions

Maze #55

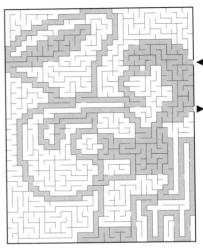

Maze #53

Maze #56

Maze #54

Solutions

Maze #57

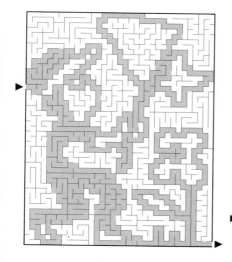

Maze #59

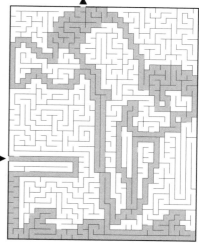

Maze #58

Maze #60

Solutions

Maze #61

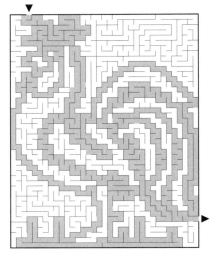

Maze #63

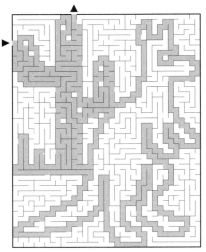

Maze #62

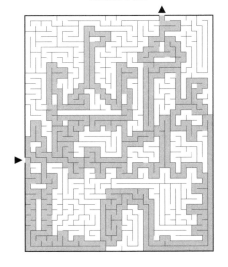

Maze #64

Solutions

Maze #67

Maze #65

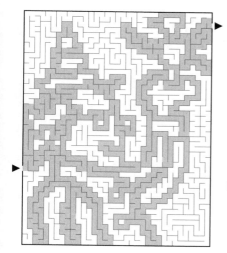

Maze #66

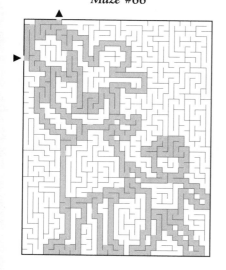

Maze #68

Solutions

Maze #70

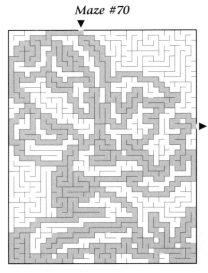

Maze #69

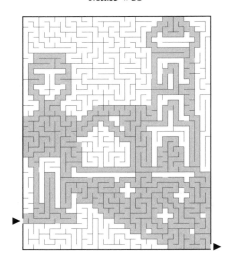

Maze #71

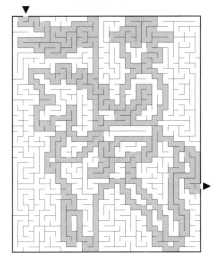

Solutions

Maze #72

Maze #73

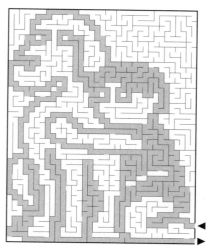

Maze #74

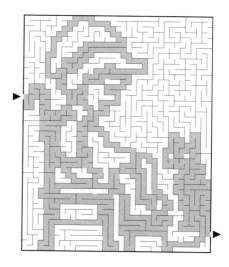

Solutions

Maze #76

Maze #75

Maze #77

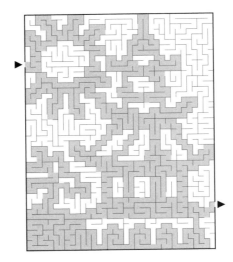